Pieces to Play

Book Four

with

Step by Step

by

Edna Mae Burnam

To Twilla Ann Ahola

CONTENTS

Book
ISBN 978-1-4234-3597-6

Book/CD
ISBN 978-1-4234-3614-0

WILLIS MUSIC

EXCLUSIVELY DISTRIBUTED BY

HAL•LEONARD®
CORPORATION
7777 W. BLUEMOUND RD. P.O. BOX 13819 MILWAUKEE, WI 53213

Visit Hal Leonard Online at
www.halleonard.com

TO THE TEACHER

The pieces in this book have been composed to correlate exactly with the Edna Mae Burnam Piano Course STEP BY STEP—Book Four. Prefixed to each piece is an indication of the exact page of STEP BY STEP—Book Four at which a selection from PIECES TO PLAY may be introduced. When the student reaches this page, he/she is ready to play with ease and understanding.

All of the pieces in this book may serve as repertoire for the student at this level.

The pieces in this book should be:

1. Perfected;
2. Memorized;
3. Played with expression and poise;
4. Kept in readiness to play for company.

Edna Mae Burnam

The student is ready to play this piece when he has reached page 8 of
Edna Mae Burnam's STEP BY STEP - Book Four.

IN THE MIDDLE OF A BRIDGE

Words and Music by
EDNA MAE BURNAM

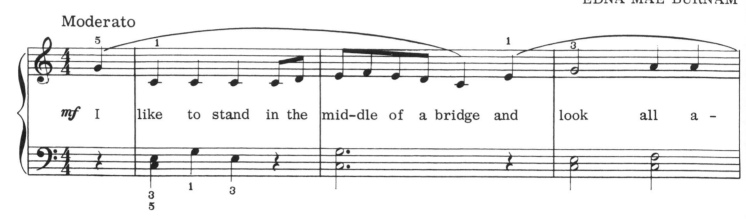

I like to stand in the mid-dle of a bridge and look all a-

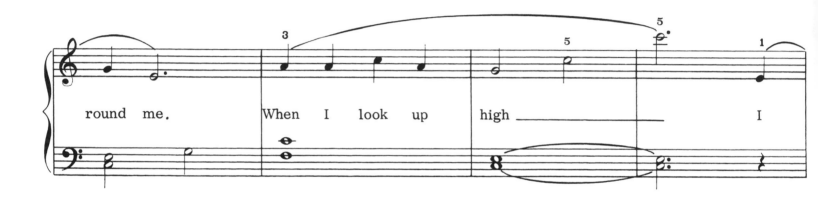

round me. When I look up high _____ I

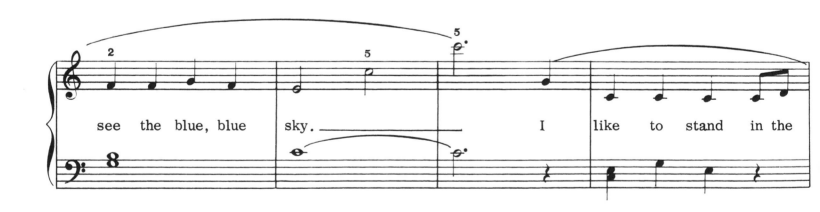

see the blue, blue sky. _____ I like to stand in the

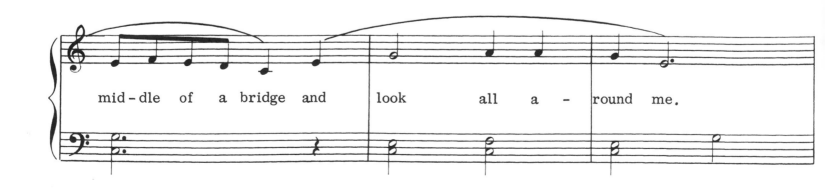

mid-dle of a bridge and look all a - round me.

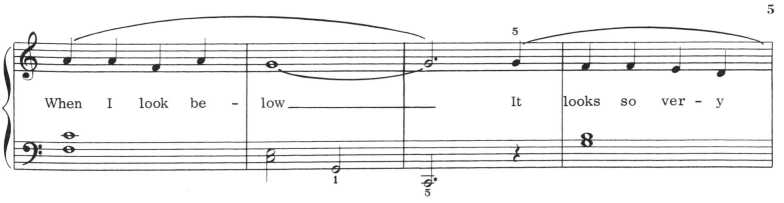

When I look be - low _____ It looks so ver - y

low. _____ I like to stand in the mid-dle of a bridge and

look all a - round me. And wheth -er high or low It's

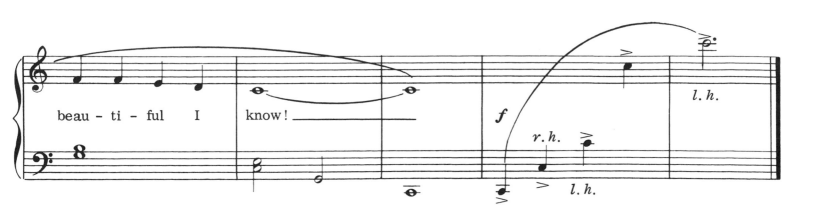

beau - ti - ful I know! _____ *f*

The student is ready to play this piece when he has reached page 13 of
Edna Mae Burnam's STEP BY STEP – Book Four.

CONTRASTS
(SMOOTHIES AND JUMP-UPS)

By EDNA MAE BURNAM

Andante "Smoothies"

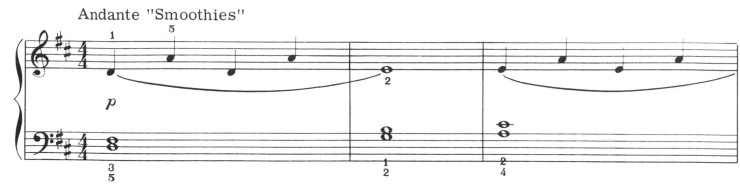

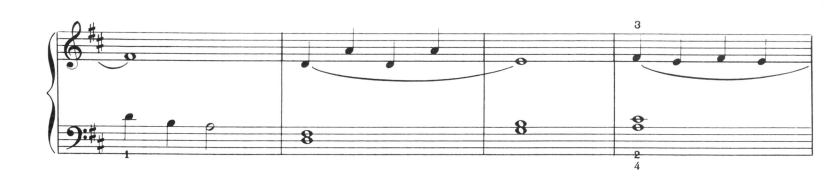

Allegretto "Jump-ups"

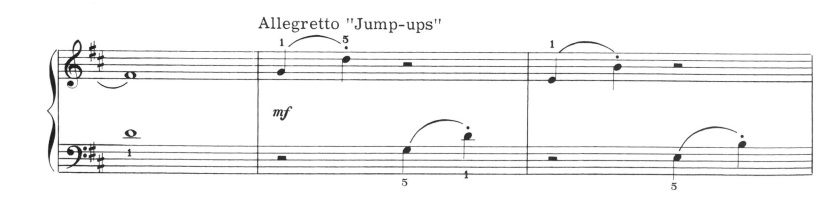

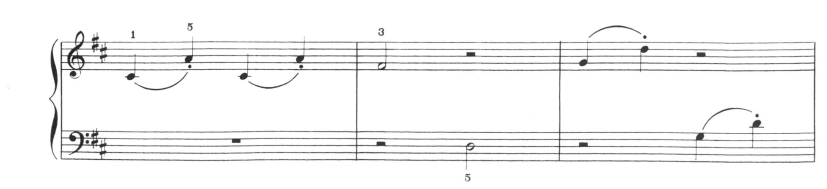

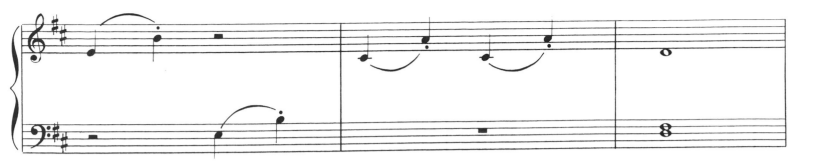

Andante "Smoothies"

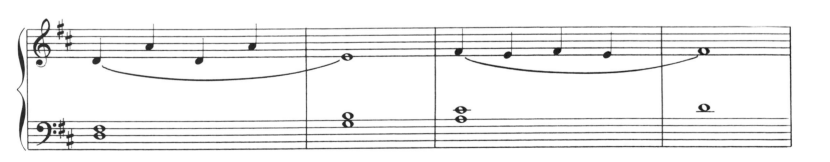

Allegretto "Jump-ups"

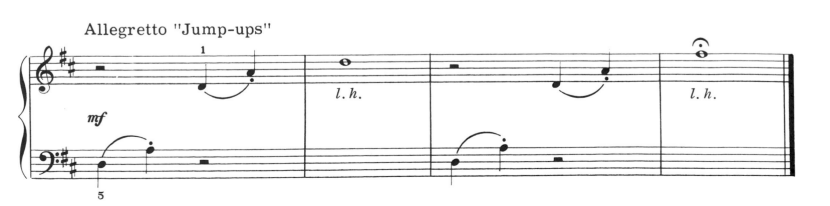

The student is ready to play this piece when he has reached page 19 of
Edna Mae Burnam's STEP BY STEP – Book Four.

TREADLE TIME TUNE

By EDNA MAE BURNAM

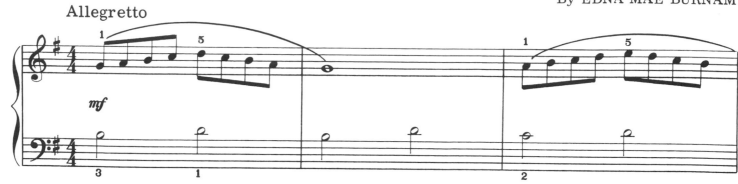

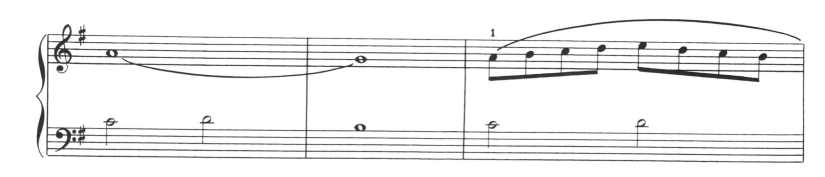

The student is ready to play this piece when he has reached page 24 of
Edna Mae Burnam's STEP BY STEP - Book Four.

I CAN HEAR AN ECHO

Words and Music by
EDNA MAE BURNAM

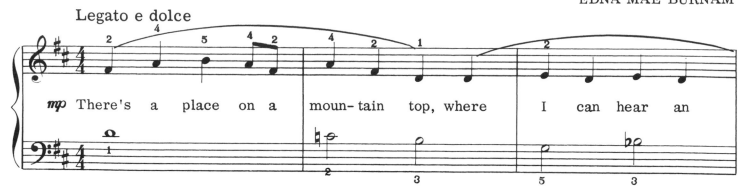

There's a place on a moun-tain top, where I can hear an

ech - o. When I call I will al - ways hear an an-swer to my

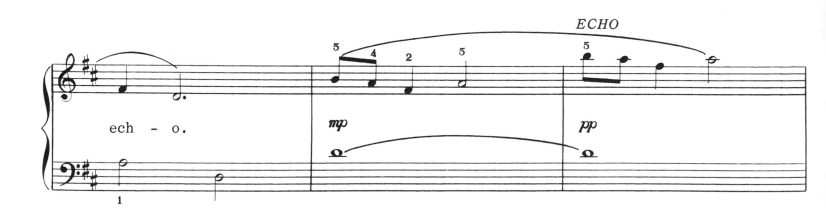

ech - o.

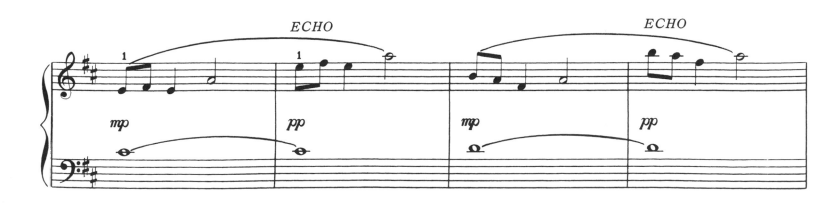

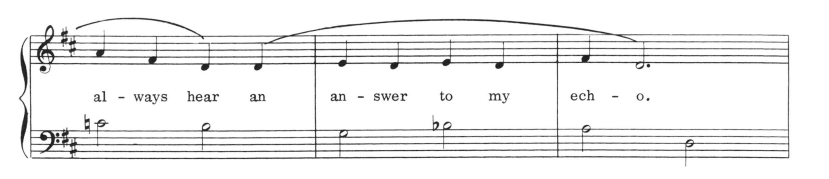

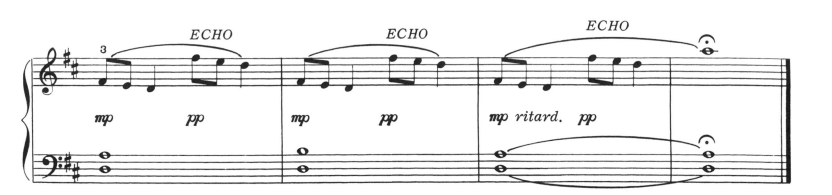

The student is ready to play this piece when he has reached page 30 of
Edna Mae Burnam's STEP BY STEP – Book Four.

SOUSAPHONE SONG

By EDNA MAE BURNAM

D.S. al Fine

The student is ready to play this piece when he has reached page 37 of
Edna Mae Burnam's STEP BY STEP – Book Four.

UNICYCLES

By EDNA MAE BURNAM

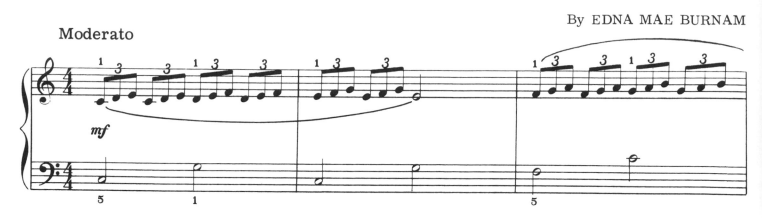

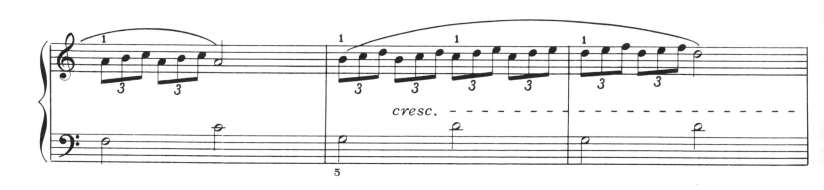

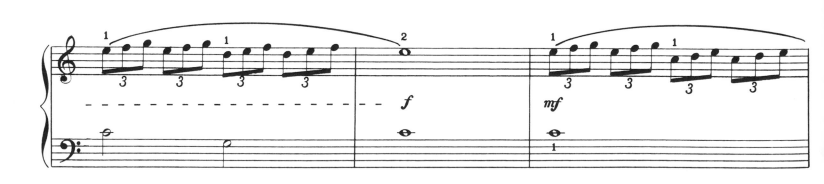

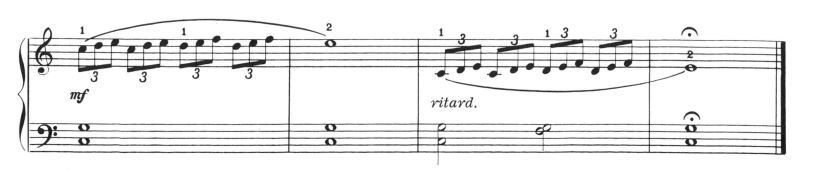

The student is ready to play this piece when he has reached page 45 of
Edna Mae Burnam's STEP BY STEP – Book Four.

A WHALE IN THE OCEAN BLUE

By EDNA MAE BURNAM

The student is ready to play this piece when he has reached page 48 of
Edna Mae Burnam's STEP BY STEP – Book Four.

BIMBO THE SCARECROW

Words and Music by
EDNA MAE BURNAM

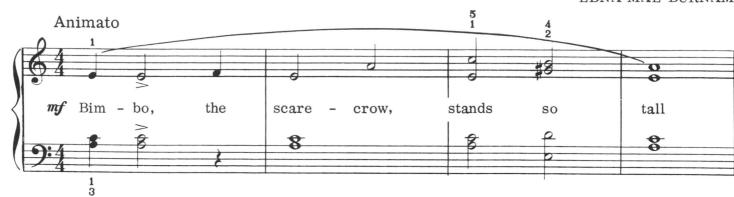

Animato

mf Bim - bo, the scare - crow, stands so tall

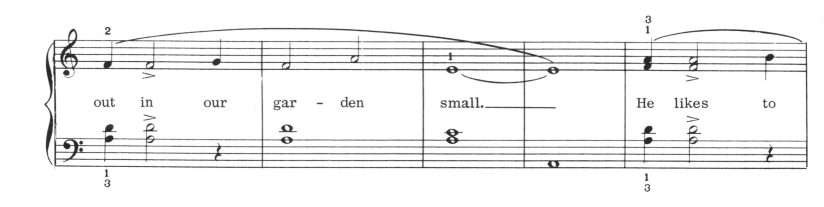

out in our gar - den small._____ He likes to

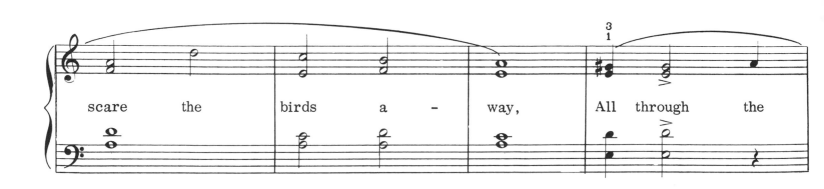

scare the birds a - way, All through the

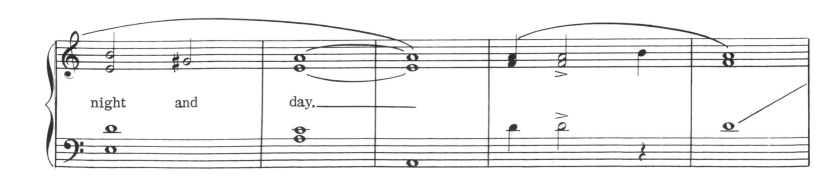

night and day._____

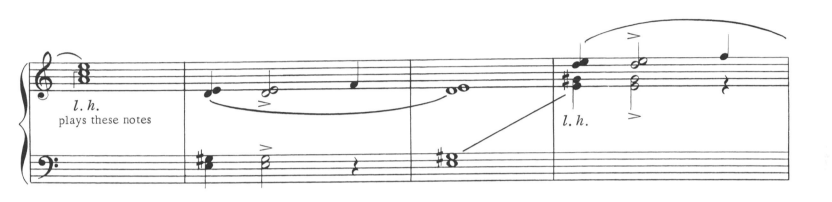

out in our gar - den small.

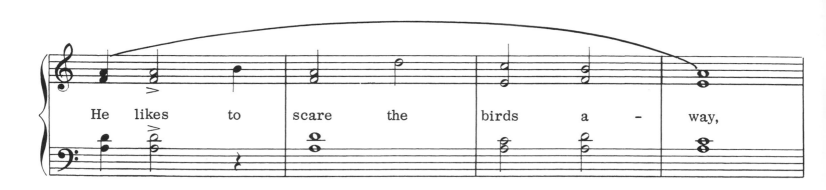

He likes to scare the birds a - way,

All through the night and day.

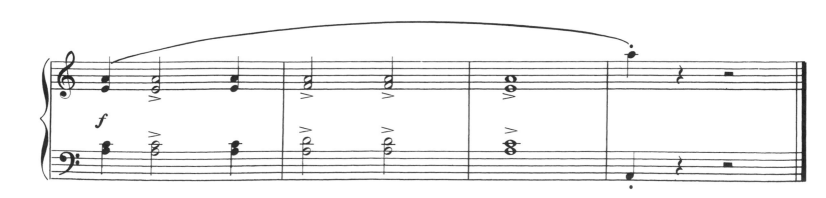

Certificate of Merit

This is to certify that

_____

has successfully completed

PIECES TO PLAY
BOOK FOUR
BY
EDNA MAE BURNAM

and is now eligible for promotion to

PIECES TO PLAY
BOOK FIVE

_____Teacher

Date _____

Edna Mae Burnam

Edna Mae Burnam (1907–2007) is one of the most respected names in piano pedagogy. She began her study of the instrument at age seven with lessons from her mother, and went on to major in piano at the University of Washington and Chico State Teacher's College in Los Angeles. In 1935, she sold "The Clock That Stopped"—one of her original compositions still in print today—to a publisher for $20. In 1937, Burnam began her long and productive association with Florence, Kentucky-based Willis Music, who signed her to her first royalty contract. In 1950, she sent manuscripts to Willis for an innovative piano series comprised of short and concise warm-up exercises—she drew stick figures indicating where the "real" illustrations should be dropped in. That manuscript, along with the original stick figures, became the best-selling *A Dozen a Day* series, which has sold more than 25 million copies worldwide; the stick-figure drawings are now icons.

Burnam followed up on the success of *A Dozen a Day* with her *Step by Step Piano Course*. This method teaches students the rudiments of music in a logical order and manageable pace, for gradual and steady progress. She also composed hundreds of individual songs and pieces, many based on whimsical subjects or her international travels. These simple, yet effective learning tools for children studying piano have retained all their charm and unique qualities, and remain in print today in the Willis catalog. Visit **www.halleonard.com** to browse all available piano music by Edna Mae Burnam.

A DOZEN A DAY
by
Edna Mae Burnam

The **A Dozen a Day** books are universally recognized as one of the most remarkable technique series on the market for all ages! Each book in this series contains short warm-up exercises to be played at the beginning of each practice session, providing excellent day-to-day training for the student. The audio CD is playable on any CD player and features fabulous backing tracks by Ric Iannone. For Windows® and Mac computer users, the CD is enhanced so you can access MIDI files for each exercise and adjust the tempo.

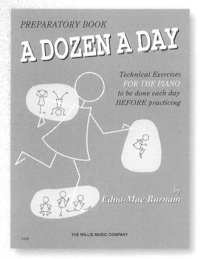

PREPARATORY BOOK
00414222   Book Only $3.95
00406476   Book/CD Pack $8.95
00406479   CD Only $9.95
00406477   Book/GM Disk Pack .. $13.95
00406480   GM Disk Only $9.95

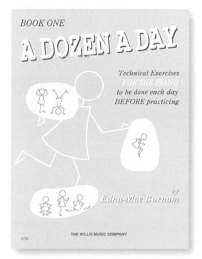

BOOK 1
00413366   Book Only $3.95
00406481   Book/CD Pack $8.95
00406483   CD Only $9.95
00406482   Book/GM Disk Pack .. $13.90
00406484   GM Disk Only $9.95

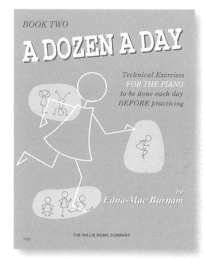

BOOK 2
00413826   Book Only $3.95
00406485   Book/CD Pack $8.95
00406487   CD Only $9.95
00406486   Book/GM Disk Pack .. $13.90
00406488   GM Disk Only $9.95

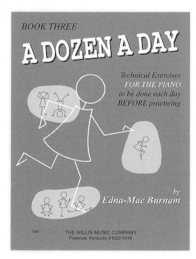

BOOK 3
00414136   Book Only $4.95
00416760   Book/CD Pack $9.95

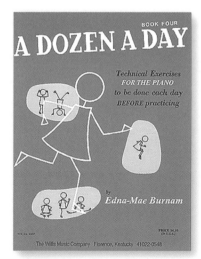

BOOK 4
00415686   Book Only $5.95
00416761   Book/CD Pack $10.95

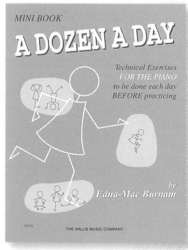

MINI BOOK
00404073   Mini Book $3.95
00406472   Book/CD Pack $8.95
00406474   CD Only $9.95
00406473   Book/GM Disk Pack .. $13.90
00406475   GM Disk Only $9.95

WILLIS MUSIC

EXCLUSIVELY DISTRIBUTED BY
HAL•LEONARD®